SURPRISINGLY SCARY!

Look Out for the DINGO!

Amy Austen

PowerKiDS press™

New York

Published in 2016 by The Rosen Publishing Group, Inc.
29 East 21st Street, New York, NY 10010

First Edition

Editor: Caitlin McAneney
Book Design: Katelyn Heinle

Photo Credits: Cover SF photo/Shutterstock.com; back cover, pp. 3, 4, 6, 8, 10–12, 14, 16, 18, 20, 22–24 (background) CAMPINCOOL/Shutterstock.com; p. 5 (dingo) John Carnemolla/Shutterstock.com; p. 5 (jackal) Pavel Zizka/Shutterstock.com; p. 7 (dingo) Jun Zhang/Shutterstock.com; p. 7 (map) ekler/Shutterstock.com; p. 9 (dingo) Nicholas Lee/Shutterstock.com; p. 9 (Carolina dog) Susan Schmitz/Shutterstock.com; p. 10 Volodymyr Burdiak/Shutterstock.com; p. 11 Natalia Pushchina/ Shutterstock.com; p. 13 © iStockphoto.com/elmvilla; p. 14 Susan Flashman/Shutterstock.com; p. 15 © iStockphoto.com/ VM Jones; p. 17 Tier Und Naturfotografie J und C Sohns/Photographer's Choice/Getty Images; p. 19 © iStockphoto.com/ Roll6; p. 21 © iStockphoto.com/timstarkey; p. 22 Auscape/Universal Images Group/Getty Images.

Library of Congress Cataloging-in-Publication Data

Austen, Amy.
Look out for the dingo! / by Amy Austen.
p. cm. — (Surprisingly scary!)
Includes index.
ISBN 978-1-4994-0878-2 (pbk.)
ISBN 978-1-4994-0894-2 (6 pack)
ISBN 978-1-4994-0938-3 (library binding)
1. Dingo — Juvenile literature. I. Austen, Amy. II. Title.
QL737.C22 A775 2016
599.77'2—d23

Manufactured in the United States of America

CPSIA Compliance Information: Batch #WS15PK: For Further Information contact Rosen Publishing, New York, New York at 1-800-237-9932

CONTENTS

DOGS ON THE LOOSE!

Do you think dogs are cute? The one at your house might be, but wild dogs can be **dangerous**! Dingoes are wild dogs that live in Australia. Dingoes also live in some places in Southeast Asia.

Dingoes may look like cuddly golden-colored dogs, but they're actually **canine** killers at the top of their food chain. Some people try to feed dingoes or play with them. Although dingo attacks on people are rare, these wild dogs can sometimes become **aggressive**. It's best to leave them alone!

SURPRISINGLY TRUE!

Scientists believe dingoes were once **domestic** dogs living in Southeast Asia. People may have brought them to Australia thousands of years ago, and they became wild.

JACKAL

There are many species, or kinds, of animals in the canine family. Wolves, jackals, and coyotes are other canines.

DINGO HABITATS

Wild dogs are found throughout the Indo-Pacific **region**. This is the area between the Indian and the Pacific Oceans. The weather here is tropical, or hot and wet. Dingoes mainly live in Australia. There, weather is hot and wet in some places, and very dry in others.

Dingoes live in many different kinds of **habitats**. Some live in the Australian desert, also called the outback. Some live in grasslands or near forests. Dingoes often travel far to find food and water.

Dingoes usually claim an area of land as their territory. It belongs to a single dingo or a pack. This is their place to hunt and make their dens.

DINGO TERRITORY

PACIFIC OCEAN

INDIAN OCEAN

AUSTRALIA

SURPRISINGLY TRUE!

Dingoes make dens in caves, empty logs, and holes left by other animals.

WHAT DOES A DINGO LOOK LIKE?

Dingoes can grow to be 4 feet (1.2 m) long, not including their tail. They usually weigh up to 35 pounds (16 kg). Their bodies are thin but strong.

Dingoes have fur that's usually golden or reddish, but sometimes black. Many have white fur on their feet and on the tip of their tail. Dingoes have great hearing. Their ears are pointed. They have long, sharp teeth for catching **prey** and tearing it into smaller pieces. Dingoes also have great senses of smell and sight.

Australian dingoes look very similar to the Carolina Dog, or American Dingo. These dogs were once wild, living in woods and swamps in the American Southeast. Today, people keep them as pets.

SURPRISINGLY TRUE!

Male dingoes are slightly larger than female dingoes.

CAROLINA DOG

LIVING IN PACKS

Dingoes are known to live alone or in groups called packs. A dingo pack usually includes a dominant, or top, male and female, plus their young. Some dingoes hunt and live alone. Others hunt alone while still belonging to a pack. Others hunt and live in a pack of up to a dozen dingoes.

SURPRISINGLY TRUE!

Hunting in a pack means grabbing more food. A pack of dingoes can take down a huge kangaroo!

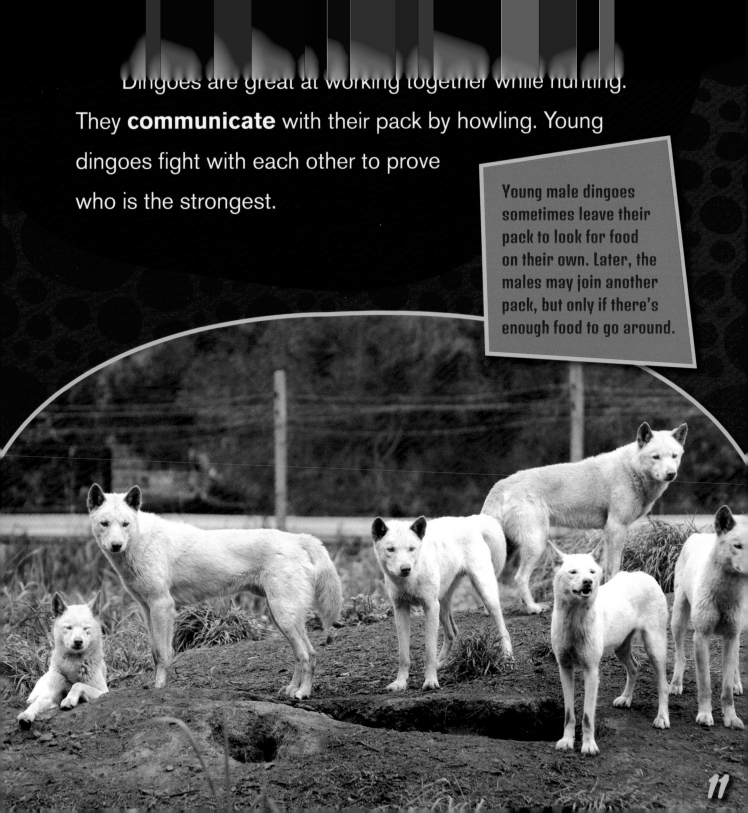

Dingoes are great at working together while hunting. They **communicate** with their pack by howling. Young dingoes fight with each other to prove who is the strongest.

Young male dingoes sometimes leave their pack to look for food on their own. Later, the males may join another pack, but only if there's enough food to go around.

TOP OF THE FOOD CHAIN

The dingo is the largest land predator in Australia. Dingoes are also known for being great hunters and fighters. They don't have any real predators that eat them. That means they're at the top of their food chain.

Dingoes are meat eaters, but also eat plants and fruits. A single dingo will hunt small animals such as lizards, birds, rats, and rabbits. A pack of dingoes can kill and eat larger animals. Dingoes are often blamed for killing farm animals, or livestock.

Dingoes are nasty killers, but they also look for and eat animals that are already dead. This makes them scavengers.

SURPRISINGLY TRUE!

If there's too much food, a dingo won't overeat. It will bury the food to eat later.

RAISING THEIR YOUNG

Dingoes **mate** for life. That means a male and female choose each other and stay together. A female dingo gives birth about once a year. Each litter has one to 10 pups.

Both parent dingoes take care of their young. They find a den for their pups to keep them safe. The parents help their young by giving them food, keeping watch over their den, and teaching them to hunt. Each year, a new group of pups joins the pack.

Older pack members and parents teach pups how to hunt, fight, and act as a pack.

DINGO ATTACKS

Dingoes rarely attack people. They more often kill and eat smaller animals. However, people still have to be careful around them. While an adult human might be able to fight off a dingo, kids could be seriously hurt.

There have been a few cases of dingoes hurting people. In 1980, dingoes killed a baby girl while her family was camping in the Australian outback. In 2001, two dingoes killed a 9-year-old boy on Fraser Island, Australia. Over the years, there have been multiple dingo attacks on this vacation island.

Fraser Island's problem with dingo attacks may have to do with people feeding and playing with the dingoes. The dingoes started to rely on the people's food.

SURPRISINGLY TRUE!

After the 2001 killing on Fraser Island, 31 dingoes were found and killed there. This angered many people who thought killing dingoes was wrong.

17

STAY AWAY!

It's important to keep people and livestock safe from dingo attacks. On Fraser Island, fencing was put around many areas where people live and vacation. This fencing is meant to keep dingoes away.

If you ever see a dingo, you should stand still with your arms folded across your chest. Back away from the dingo slowly. Calmly call for help. Don't wave your arms or run. That might make the dingo think you want a fight.

It's important to never feed dingoes. Never leave food out at a picnic. Dingoes might fight for the food.

SURPRISINGLY TRUE!

A dog fence was built across southern Australia to keep dingoes out of farmland. It's nearly 3,400 miles (5,472 km) long and is the longest fence in the world!

DINGOES IN DANGER

Dingoes are endangered, or at risk of **extinction**. Crocodiles and snakes sometimes kill dingoes. However, human attacks on dingoes are their greatest risk.

People hunt dingoes because they think they're dangerous or just for sport. Dingoes are often treated as pests. Farmers are allowed to kill dingoes that come near their livestock. Another reason dingoes may go extinct is because dingoes started mating with people's pet dogs. This makes more half-dingoes and fewer pure dingoes.

SURPRISINGLY TRUE!

When dingoes mate with other dogs, the result is called a dingo-dog hybrid. These dogs can be dangerous because many are bigger than normal dingoes.

One way people can save the
dingo is by fencing in pure
dingoes with each other.
These areas would be safe for
dingoes and would allow them
to mate with dingoes only.

SAVING THE DINGO

If you're expecting a cute dog, a wild dingo can be surprisingly scary to run into. It's best to stay away and admire this great hunter from afar!

Humans and dingoes have a long history together. Native people of Australia, called Aborigines, kept dingoes as pets. Aborigines told stories and made drawings of dingoes for thousands of years. Now, some scientists believe dingoes could be extinct in 50 years. It's our duty to practice safety around wild animals like the dingo, while keeping their species alive and well!

This Aborigine cave painting is more than 15,000 years old. It shows us that dingoes have been around a very long time.

GLOSSARY

aggressive: Showing a readiness to attack.

canine: Having to do with a dog.

communicate: To share ideas and feelings through sounds and motions.

dangerous: Unsafe.

domestic: Raised for use by people.

extinction: The death of all members of a species.

habitat: The natural home for plants, animals, and other living things.

mate: To join together as a pair.

prey: An animal hunted by other animals for food.

region: A large area that has things in common.

INDEX

WEBSITES

Due to the changing nature of Internet links, PowerKids Press has developed an online list of websites related to the subject of this book. This site is updated regularly. Please use this link to access the list: www.powerkidslinks.com/surp/ding